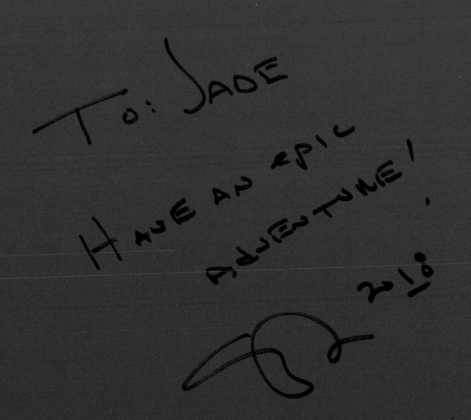

To: Jade

Have an epic
Adventure!
2018

Eli and Mort's Epic Adventures Steamboat

About this project

The idea for Eli and Mort's Epic Adventures Series came from the joy we experienced watching our kids ski, snowboard and have the time of their lives growing up in the mountains. We wanted to share that joy and the beauty of the mountains with the world. We decided to write a series of books through the eyes of a child on an epic adventure -- a series of books for adventuring kids like you! This is the third book in the Series, "Eli and Mort's Epic Adventures Steamboat."

When considering the concept we imagined what a child might see and feel when they stood at the top of the mountain about to take the first run of the day, and thought, 'Who better qualified to illustrate the book than the children that live here'? As a result, we agreed that the background illustrations should be drawn by the children of Steamboat Springs.

About the characters

Eli, a 5-year-old boy, and his pal Mort the Moose are the best of friends exploring the world together. When others are around Mort is a stuffed moose but to Eli, Mort is his best friend and partner in fun. In this book, they are experiencing all that Steamboat Springs has to offer.

Eli and Mort are dedicated to the loves of our lives,
Josh, Heath & Will.

Enjoy!

Created by Elyssa Pallai and Ken Nager
Published by Resort Books Ltd.
Background illustrations by the children of the Yampa Valley
Character Illustrations by Eduardo Paj
Background Cover image by James Dickson

Printed in Korea
September 2015

Thank you

We love our friends in Steamboat Springs. Mort and I think you are AWESOME! Special thanks to Eduardo Paj for making us look so good, Nicole Magistro from the Bookworm who inspired us to write this, Brent and Barb Bingham at PhotoFX and Brenda Himelfarb and Diane Pallai for making sure what we wrote was what we meant to write. Thank you to Shannon Lukens for providing several photos for creative direction. www.lukensmountainmedia.com. "Hooray!" to all of the AWESOME children who illustrated this book and their parents. Special thanks to the Steamboat Springs Arts Council for their ongoing support in helping us reach the world.

Thank you to Steamboat Ski & Resort Corporation. Steamboat trademarks are used with permission.

Visit **eliandmort.com** to order our latest adventure, check out our events or to just say, "Hi!"

A portion of the proceeds of this book go to the Steamboat Springs Arts Council.

The Illustrators

Eli and Mort would like to thank the AMAZING local children, ages 7 to 18, that illustrated the backgrounds! Below are some of their favorite things to do in Steamboat. What's yours?

D

Courtney Vargas

Steamboat Springs Middle School
11 years old
Favorite: Playing soccer & ski all day!

I

Leilani Ward

Steamboat Springs Middle School
12 years old
Favorite: Skiing & tubing

E

Tanner Stover

Steamboat Springs High School
17 years old
Favorite: Skiing, ice skating & go to community events

J

Grant Janka

Steamboat Springs High School
16 years old
Favorite: Watching wildlife

A

James Dickson

Steamboat Springs High School
18 years old
Favorite: Skiing

F

Athena Marsh

Steamboat Springs High School
16 years old
Favorite: Snowboarding & swimming

K

Preston Anderson

Steamboat Springs High School
18 years old
Favorite: Snowboarding, hiking & tubing

B

Suzy Magill

Soda Creek Elementary School
10 years old
Favorite: Skiing & Winter Carnival

G

Isaak Sanders

Soda Creek Elementary School
9 years old
Favorite: Skiing

L

Ella Walker

Soda Creek Elementary School
10 years old
Favorite: Ski & playing soccer

C

Brie Bunker

Soda Creek Elementary School
8 years old
Favorite: Skiing with family

H

Ava Thorp

Emerald Mountain School
7 years old
Favorite: Riding horses

M

Alison Apostle

Soda Creek Elementary School
10 years old
Favorite: Skiing, tubing & walking downtown

N

Gaven Mellen

South Route Elementary
11 years old
Favorite: Bowling, shopping & skiing

T

Mickinley McAtee

Steamboat Springs High School
15 years old
Favorite: Walking Spring Creek Trail, sitting by the river and reading

Z

Finley Parker

Home Schooled
7 years old
Favorite: Skiing

O

Keelan Vargas

Steamboat Springs High School
15 years old
Favorite: Playing soccer & hiking

U

Julia McCarthy

Steamboat Springs Middle School
13 years old
Favorite: Skiing and eating ice cream

Outtakes

Lyla Yukiko Baker

Soda Creek Elementary School
7 years old
Favorite: Skiing

P

Riq Rogers

Steamboat Springs Middle School
11 years old
Favorite: Skiing, swimming, skateboarding and bike riding

V

Shea Speer

Soda Creek Elementary School
7 years old
Favorite: Ice skating

Outtakes

Allie Keefe

Soda Creek Elementary School
10 years old
Favorite: Skiing & hanging with my friends

Q

Sydney O'Hare

Steamboat Springs Middle School
12 years old
Favorite: Skiing on Mount Werner

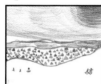

W

Ryley Seibel

Steamboat Springs Middle School
12 years old
Favorite: Hiking

Outtakes

Annie Martin

Steamboat Springs High School
16 years old
Favorite: Hiking

R

Heidi Andre

North Routt Community Charter School
10 years old
Favorite: Skiing

X

Dane Bessette

Steamboat Springs High School
16 years old
Favorite: Downhill biking

Outtakes

Sophie Picking

Soda Creek Elementary School
10 years old
Favorite: Playing hockey with my brother & playing with friends

S

Brooke Bunker

Soda Creek Elementary School
7 years old
Favorite: Building a snowman with my family

Y

Dylan Ciraldo Freese

Soda Creek Elementary School
10 years old
Favorite: Play with friends, dance, play piano, snowboard

A is for our Wild West ski **Adventure** in Steamboat Springs. My dad told us that Steamboat was full of cowboys, pioneers, Olympians, hot springs and really friendly people. So the night before my stepmom, dad, li'l sis, Mort my moose and I left for our adventure, we packed our cowboy hats, skis, bathing suits and our very own gold soccer medals. We were ready for our Wild West, Olympic adventure in Steamboat!

B is for **Hot Air Balloons**. On our first morning, Mort and I woke up to gigantic hot air balloons floating way up high in the Colorado big sky. I thought someone must be celebrating a birthday! Mort thought so too. So we sang "Happy Birthday to You!"

suzy Magill

C is for **Winter Carnival**. My stepmom told us that one of Steamboat's pioneers, Carl Howelsen, loved winter sports so much that he wanted to have a party to celebrate them. So Carl created the Winter Carnival in 1914. At the carnival, I decided to try my luck at skijoring, a sport where a horse pulls a skier with a rope. "Yee-haw!" I hollered as I flew over the jump.

D is for **Cowboy Downhill**. Cowboys with hats and chaps stampeded, galloped, bucked and did tricks on their way down the mountain. One cowboy flew past us and lost his hat. Mort picked it up and gave it back. "Thank you young moose," the cowboy said. Mort was pleased with himself. I was pleased with Mort too.

E is for **Elk Mountain**. Elk Mountain is the shape of a sleeping giant you can see from everywhere in Steamboat Springs. According to a legend, the sleeping giant protects Steamboat Springs from danger. That made Mort feel safe. We saw a cloud puff from the top of the mountain so we knew the giant was snoring!

F is for **Fuzzywig's Candy Factory**. "Have we gone to candy heaven?" I asked Mort as we entered the sea of red, yellow, green, and pink colored candy walls, boxes of squishy Swedish fish and gobstoppers the size of baseballs. Mort liked the sweet ones and I liked the sour ones. This worked out well because it meant we didn't have to share our candy with each other.

G is for the **Glades** of trees. Swish, swish was the sound our
skis made as we swooshed through the powder in the glades
of the tall Aspen trees. "Whoopee!" I yelled. Mort laughed,
"Yepa-doodle-do!" as we "crushed it" through the trees.

H is for **Horses** that run and play in the snow. My dad says that there are a lot of ranchers who live in Steamboat Springs and the horses they ride are their trusty companions.

Da-da-dum, da-da-dum, was the sound we were making as my li'l sis, Mort and I galloped through the snowdrifts, tossing puffs of snow in the air and holding on as tight as we could.

I is for the old fashioned Ice Cream Soda Fountain at Lyon's Drugstore. I ordered a vanilla malted milk shake. Mort wanted a root beer float. We ate our ice cream so fast our brains froze. I held Mort's forehead until he felt better.

J is for ski **Jumps** at Howelsen Hill where future Olympians fly in the air, sometimes upside down and around again until their skis hit the ground. "I am so going to try that," I told Mort. I practiced with Mort, flipping him over and over again in my arms imagining him as the next great freeskier.

K is for **Billy Kidd** the alpine skiing legend. Mort and I couldn't wait to ski down the mountain with Billy, which my stepmom told me, is something you can do almost every day. After skiing with Billy we asked him if he would take a selfie with us. It was our first selfie with an Olympian. Mort thought that was AWESOME. I thought so too.

L is for **Lil' Rodeo Terrain Park**
where we slid over the boxes
with our skis just like the
skiers at Howelsen Hill. Mort and I
caught huge air off of the half-pipe,
held our bodies tight and stuck the
landings! Yahoo!

M is for **Main Street.** Steamboat looks just like an old Western Town with a wide street for horses and buggies and gun-smoked sheriffs. Mort and I imagined our family dressed up like cowboys. It made us laugh.

N is for **Night Skiing**. Skiing during the day was AWESOME but night skiing was even more fun. Mount Werner was named after Buddy Werner, a famous Olympian from Steamboat. We thought Buddy must have practiced all day AND all night. So we did too.

O is for **Olympians** who believe in making the world a better place through sport. Steamboat Springs has produced more winter Olympians than any other town in North America. My stepmom said it must be something in the water...so Mort and I drank lots and lots of it.

P is for **Powder**. Steamboat's powder is so light and fluffy it floats and twinkles in the air like champagne. Steamboat has lots of it. Mort and I loved trying big tricks in the drifty snow and watching the flakes twinkle in the sun.

Q is for **Quickdraw** run which is just the right speed for Mort and me. We liked the name because we pretended to quick draw our play cowboy pistols at the start. "Bang bang, bang bang," we'd call out together making the sound of cowboys playing as we pointed our fingers.

R is for Johnny B. Good's **Restaurant.** Mort and I liked the Haley Burger the best. On Johnny B. Good's menu it says "It's the kids favorite. Haley says so." So we believed her. The walls were also covered with pictures of movie stars Mort and I had never heard of, but my stepmom and dad knew who they were.

S is for **Strawberry Park Hot Springs**. Strawberry Park is a magical place of pools of hot spring water. Mort, my li'l sis and I would hop from the cold river, to the medium pool to the REALLY hot pool. We liked feeling our skin tingle as the water got hotter and hotter. My stepmom just stayed in the REALLY hot one. I yelled, "Yippee" as I did another cannon ball into the water.

T is for **Thunderhead** at the top of the Gondola. Mort, my li'l sis and I loved taking the Gondola up and down the mountain. During ski school we were given chocolate chip cookies that we tried to make last until we got to Thunderhead at the very top of the Gondola.

U is for **Up Top** of the mountain where we visited the Storm Peak Laboratory. My dad told Mort, me and my li'l sis that scientists study the atmosphere from there. My dad explained that the sky was made of different layers, just like you see in a cake. And that is the atmosphere! My li'l sis and I watched the weather balloon float away until it disappeared into the cake layer in the sky.

V is for big sky **View**. Steamboat had the biggest sky of any town we had ever visited. The sky looked like it went on forever and ever. Mort and I would sometimes sit at the top of the mountain wondering why the sky looked even BIGGER here than it did at home.

Shea

W is for **Wildlife**. Steamboat Springs is full of really amazing animals. We saw deer, elk and visited some of Mort's cousins, the wild moose who were eating and relaxing in the trees.

X is for **Sunshine eXpress**. We liked the Sunshine Express because it took us to Wally World, the area on Mount Werner that was especially fun for kids. Mort, my li'l sis and I knew we needed to practice if we wanted to be Olympians. We turned back and forth on our skis, over and over again.

Y is for **Yampa River**, the river that runs through Steamboat. Mort and I tried out fly fishing from one of the Yampa River bridges. The fishing line made a swooooosh, wooooosh noise as we swung the pole back and forth. Mort and I caught a lot of snowballs while fishing, but no fish.

Z is for **ZZZ** the sound Mort and I made at the end of our last big day in Steamboat Springs. We can't wait for our next adventure!

FINLEYPARKER

Outtakes

There was so much more to do in Steamboat.

Lyla yukiko Baker

Allie Keefe

See you in ASPEN
on our next adventure!

Check out our
other adventures at
www.eliandmort.com

Beaver Creek

Vail

Vail-en Espanol

Breckenridge

Learn to Snowboard